Creating the Band

An Accounting Simulation for
Peachtree®, QuickBooks®, and Microsoft® Excel

By Beth Kane CPA MBA

Howard W. Rankin, MBA, Contributing Author

D1370213

THOMSON

SOUTH-WESTERN

Australia · Canada · Mexico · Singapore · Spain · United Kingdom · United States

THOMSON

SOUTH-WESTERN

Creating the Band
An Accounting Simulation for *Peachtree®*, *QuickBooks®*, and *Microsoft®* Excel
Beth Kane

VP/Editorial Director:
Jack W. Calhoun

VP/Editor-in-Chief:
Karen Schmohe

Acquisitions Editor:
Marilyn Hornsby

Project Manager:
Carol Sturzenberger

Consulting Editor:
Dianne S. Rankin

VP/Director of Marketing:
Carol Volz

Marketing Manager:
Courtney Schulz

Marketing Coordinator:
Angela Russo

Production Editor:
Diane Bowdler

Production Manager:
Patricia Matthews Boies

Manufacturing Coordinator:
Kevin Kluck

Production House:
settingPace, LLC

Cover Design:
Stratton Design

Cover Image:
© Getty Images

Internal Designer:
settingPace, LLC

Printer:
Banta
Harrisonburg, VA

ASIA (including India)
Thomson Learning
5 Shenton Way
#01-01 UIC Building
Singapore 068808

AUSTRALIA/NEW ZEALAND
Thomson Learning Australia
102 Dodds Street
Southbank, Victoria 3006
Australia

LATIN AMERICA
Thomson Learning
Seneca, 53
Colonia Polanco
11560 Mexico
D.F. Mexico

CANADA
Thomson Nelson
1120 Birchmount Road
Toronto, Ontario
Canada M1K 5G4

UK/EUROPE/MIDDLE EAST/AFRICA
Thomson Learning
High Holborn House
50-51 Bedford Road
London WC1R 4LR
United Kingdom

SPAIN (includes Portugal)
Thomson Paraninfo
Calle Magallanes, 25
28015 Madrid, Spain

To My Family

I would like to thank my terrific husband Jimmy and
my wonderful children Kyle and Kacy for their inspiration,
support, and encouragement during the writing of this simulation.

I would also like to thank my sister, Michelle True, for her support
and help with technical questions as I tackled this project.

To the Users of My Simulation

I hope you view this simulation as a representation of
how in life, you can follow your convictions and passions
to success and give back to the projects that inspire you.

Beth Kane

TABLE OF CONTENTS

PREFACE

Creating the Band: An Accounting Simulation for Peachtree®, QuickBooks®, and Microsoft® Excel is designed to give you realistic experience in keeping accounting records for a small business. While completing this practice set, you will work as an accountant for CTB. CTB is a band whose members have formed a business partnership. The band gives live performances and sells music CDs. You will record varied transactions such as initial investments of capital, routine billing and payments, adjusting entries, and closing entries. You will also prepare financial statements for the business.

You will need this student textbook, a company data file, and software for recording transactions to complete this practice set. You will also need a good working knowledge of basic accounting concepts.

Organization of the Student Text

This student textbook is organized in two sections, *Introduction* and *Transactions*. The *Introduction* describes your role as an accountant for CTB. The software and data files that may be used to complete this practice set are discussed. Background information about the company is also included in the *Introduction*.

The *Transactions* section of this book contains the information you will use to keep accounting records for the company. General instructions and specific information related to the software being used are included. Check figures are provided to help you monitor your progress at various points. Software Tips, Accounting Tips, and FYI boxes provide helpful information for completing transactions. Deposit ticket forms are also included in the *Transactions* section.

Software and Data Files

This practice set may be completed using the following programs:
◆ *Peachtree® Complete Accounting Educational Version 2004* or higher
◆ *QuickBooks® Pro 2004* or higher
◆ *Microsoft® Excel* version 5.0 or higher

The data CD-ROM provided in the back of the textbook includes data files for all three programs. You will use the file that works for your software. You should have a good working knowledge of the software you will use before completing this practice set, which is not designed to teach you to use the software.

Instructor's Materials

An Instructor's Manual is available for use with *Creating the Band: An Accounting Simulation for Peachtree®, QuickBooks®, and Microsoft® Excel*. The manual contains an overview of the practice set, teaching suggestions, check figures, and an audit test. Sample solutions are included for financial statements, deposit tickets, journal/general ledger reports, and the audit test.

INTRODUCTION

Welcome to *Creating the Band: An Accounting Simulation for Peachtree®, QuickBooks®, and Microsoft® Excel.* This practice set is designed to give you realistic experience in keeping accounting records for a small business. You will work as an accountant for CTB, a group that has just formed a business partnership.

The band members will count on you to keep their accounting records up to date and in proper order. You will record transactions using common business documents such as checks and invoices as sources of information. Because this is a new business, you will record transactions related to forming a company, such as the initial capital investment of each partner.

As the band becomes popular, it will record and sell music CDs. You will record transactions related to merchandise (CD) sales. You will make the appropriate entries to adjust inventories. You will also handle transactions for income the band receives for live performances and from music videos.

Other transactions involve the routine operation of the business. Checks must be created to pay for rent, utilities, and other expenses. Depreciation must be recorded on office equipment and furniture. Payroll must be computed and checks issued to employees. As the band becomes successful, partners will withdraw money from the business. You will record transactions for these common business activities.

Your work for the band will span an entire year. You will complete the end-of-fiscal-period work, such as making adjusting and closing entries. You will also prepare financial statements, such as an income statement and balance sheet.

Organization of the Text

This student textbook is organized in two sections, *Introduction* and *Transactions.* The *Introduction* describes your role as an accountant for CTB. The organization of the text is described in this section. The software and data files that may be used to complete this practice set are discussed. Background information about the company is also included in the *Introduction*.

The *Transactions* section of this book contains the information you will use to keep accounting records for the company. General instructions and specific information related to the software being used are provided. This section also includes:

◆ A transaction number and date for each transaction

◆ Notes describing each transaction

◆ A source document for most transactions

◆ Information about changes in the structure of the business or about its activities

◆ Check figures to help you verify that your work is correct

Software and Data Files

This practice set may be completed using the following programs:

◆ *Peachtree® Complete Accounting Educational Version 2004* or higher

◆ *QuickBooks® Pro 2004* or higher

◆ *Microsoft® Excel* version 5.0 or higher

The data CD provided in the back of the textbook includes data files for all three programs. The data folder or filenames are:

Peachtree folder:	**CTB** *Peachtree*
QuickBooks file:	**CTB.qbw**
Excel file:	**CTB.xls**

You should have a good working knowledge of the software you will use before completing this practice set, which is not designed to teach you to use the software.

Company Background

The members of the CTB band formed a partnership on January 2 of the current year. The owners of the business are Kyle Jaffe, Kacy Jaffe, Joey Yap, and Bernadette Yap. All the band members are in their early twenties.

The owners hired you on January 2 of the current year to work part-time taking care of their accounting needs. You are working as a contractor for the band, not as an employee. (Later, however, you will become a full-time employee.)

The owners are musicians who have been friends since childhood. They have been playing together as a group for the past few years. The band plays at clubs locally in Crystal Lake, the town where the members live. They have been building a strong following over the past two years.

Kacy has a strong interest in business. Because of this, she has taken college business courses online over the past two years and will act as the financial officer for the band.

The band has been approached by music promoters regarding recording a CD. The band members have rejected these offers, however, because they wish to maintain artistic control over the type of music they produce and the band's image.

The band members have worked day jobs for the past few years to save enough money to record and produce their own CD. To achieve this goal, they formed their business at the beginning of the year. Their parents will loan them the money to pay their estimated operating expenses for the first year. The band members plan to rent a studio where they can practice.

TRANSACTIONS

Because you are working part-time for the band, you will not work for them every day. You will record several transactions on each day that you work (two or three days each month). Use the date given with each transaction when making entries, not the date on the related source document. Use the current year in dates for all transactions. For example, Transactions 1 through 3 should be dated January 3 of the current year. This is your first day at work for the band.

Instructions for *Peachtree*® Users

To complete this practice set, you should already have a good working knowledge of *Peachtree*® *Complete Accounting Educational Version 2004* or higher. You should also have a good working knowledge of the accounting cycle, including adjusting and closing entries.

The company data folder **CTB** *Peachtree* is for your use in completing this practice set. This data folder can be found on the data CD within your textbook. Accounts for the company have been created in this company data folder. The chart of accounts is also shown on page 13 of this textbook.

Copying the Data Folder

Before you begin recording transactions, you must copy the data folder **CTB** *Peachtree* to a working folder on a hard drive or a network drive. Your instructor will tell you where to create your working folder.

Copy the folder **CTB** *Peachtree* into your working folder. Rename the folder **CTB XX** (where **XX** represents your initials or a code number assigned by your instructor). Now you can start *Peachtree* and begin work.

At the beginning of each work session, choose *Open Company* from the *File* menu. When a *Peachtree Accounting* box appears, warning you that this action will close the company, click *OK*. Browse to your working folder. Choose and open your **CTB XX** folder.

At the end of each work session, you should close the company. To do so, choose *Open Company* from the *File* menu. When a *Peachtree Accounting* box appears, warning you that this action will close the company, click *OK*. This will close your file. Click *Cancel* to close the *Open Company* dialog box.

Using Peachtree to Record Transactions

Record the transactions and create the reports under the heading for each month on pages 14–79. Read the following paragraphs for more detailed instructions.

Software Tip

Your instructor may want you to rename the company by adding your name or initials. This will help identify reports that you print. To do so, start *Peachtree*. Open the company **CTB**. Open the *Company Information* window (under the *Maintain* menu). Change the company name to **CTB XX** (where **XX** represents your initials or your name).

Use the correct date indicated by each transaction. Use the current year in all dates. Key the document number (include *Check* or *Invoice*) or transaction number (include *Transaction*) in the *Description* or *Memo* field. For adjusting entries, key **Adjusting** in the *Description* field. For closing entries, key **Closing** in the *Description* field.

You can print a General Ledger Trial Balance report (under the *General Ledger* option of the *Reports* menu) as of March 31, June 30, September 30, and December 31 before adjusting entries. You can use these Trial Balance reports to compare your *Peachtree* balances to the check figures on pages 82 and 83.

After you have completed the last transaction for June (Transaction 19), print a General Ledger report. The General Ledger report can be found under the *General Ledger* option of the *Reports* menu. Use January 1 and June 30 of the current year for the *From* and *To* dates. Print the report in landscape orientation.

When you view and print the financial statements, use the <Standard> Income Stmnt report and the <Standard> Balance Sheet report. The <Standard> Income Stmnt report should be printed before closing entries are made.

You will need to fill out deposit tickets for the checks received in the transactions. (Blank deposit tickets are on pages 84–87.) Fill out one deposit ticket for each work day on which you have one or more checks. You will not print deposit tickets from *Peachtree Complete Accounting*. Enter all dates using the full month, day, and current year (January 1, 20--). Enter the check number next to the amount.

You will use different windows and features of *Peachtree* to record the various transactions. The window you should use for each type of transaction is listed below.

1. Use the *General Journal Entry* window (from the *Tasks* menu) to record transactions that do not involve cash payments, sales on account, receipts on account, purchases on account, or payments on account. Key the transaction number (include *Transaction*) in the *Reference* field.

   Transaction 1 (recording the cashier's check to start CTB) is an example of an entry that should be recorded in the *General Journal Entry* window. Adjusting and closing entries should also be made in the *General Journal Entry* window.

2. Use the *Write Checks* window (from the *Tasks* menu) for cash payments that are not made on account. Start with Check No. 1101. Be sure to enter the correct date using the current year.

   Transaction 4, the rent payment to Dan and Dee Properties, is an example of a transaction for which you would use the *Write Checks* window. Key **1101** in the *Check Number* field.

   Check the *Vendor ID* drop-down list. If Dan and Dee Properties is on the list, click on the *ID*. If Dan and Dee Properties is not on the list, key **Dan and Dee Properties** in the *Name* field of the *Pay to the Order of* box. Enter the remaining information for the check and click *Save*.

Repeat this process for all remaining cash payment transactions. Number the checks in sequential order.

3. Use the *Sales/Invoicing* window (from the *Tasks* menu) to invoice for shows (live performances) or the sale of CDs. Enter the correct invoice number and date. When a *Peachtree Accounting* message box appears with a warning regarding the customer credit limit, click *OK*.

   Select the customer from the *Customer* drop-down list. Select *Bill to Address* from the *Ship To* drop-down list. Enter the quantity sold in the *Quantity* field. Select the correct item from the drop-down list. The *Description* field is filled in by *Peachtree*. For the *Shows* item, the *Unit Price* and the *Amount* fields are completed by *Peachtree*. For the *CDs* item, you must fill in the *Unit Price* field and click in the *Amount* field to calculate *CD Sales* dollars.

   Repeat the process for all remaining sales to customers. Note: If the transaction date is earlier than the current date by more than the number of days in the payment terms (30 days), *Past Due* will show on the invoice. Disregard this.

4. Use the *Receipts* window (from the *Tasks* menu) to record receipts on account. Choose the customer from the *Customer ID* drop-down list. Key the CTB invoice in the *Reference* field and the customer's check number in the *Receipt Number* field. Be sure to place a check mark next to the invoice you wish to receive payment against.

   For Transaction 37, a check is received from Vallejo Music for $980,000 ($1,000,000.00 minus the 2% discount). The transaction is recorded on August 30, but the check is dated August 23. When you enter the August 30 transaction date, the invoice shows a balance due of $1,000,000.00.

   Because the check was received within the discount period, you should manually apply the discount. To enter the discount amount, key **20,000.00** in the *Discount* field and click in the *Amount Paid* field. The net amount ($980,000.00) should show in the field. Save the receipt.

5. Use the *Purchases/Receive Inventory* window (under the *Tasks* menu) to record purchases on account. Be sure to use the correct date. Key the vendor invoice number in the *Invoice No.* field. Choose the vendor from the drop down list. The payment terms are automatically entered by *Peachtree*.

   Enter the invoice quantity in the *Quantity* field. Leave the *Item* field blank. Enter the description from the vendor invoice in the *Description* field. Key the price per unit in the *Unit Price* field. Click in the *Amount* field to calculate the invoice. If the data are all correct, click *Save*.

6. Use the *Payments* window (under the *Tasks* menu) to make payments on account. Choose the vendor from the *Vendor ID* drop-down list. Key the next sequential check number in the *Check Number* field. Be sure to use the correct date.

Key the vendor invoice number in the *Memo* field. (Hint: Look in the *Invoice* field on the bottom half of the window to see the invoice number.) Place a check mark next to the invoice you wish to pay. Click *Save* to save the transaction.

Instructions for *QuickBooks*® *Pro 2004* Users

To complete this practice set, you should already have a good working knowledge of *QuickBooks*® *Pro 2004* or higher. You should also have a good working knowledge of the accounting cycle, including adjusting and closing entries.

The company data file **CTB.qbw** is for your use in completing this practice set. This data file can be found in the **CTB** *QuickBooks* folder on the data CD within your textbook. Accounts for the company have been created in this company file. The chart of accounts is also shown on page 13 of this textbook.

Copying the Data File

Before you begin recording transactions, you must copy the data file to a working folder. *QuickBooks*® *Pro 2004* will not open the company data file from a CD-ROM. You must copy the data file **CTB.qbw** to a working folder on a hard drive, a floppy disk, or a network drive so the file can be opened. Your instructor will tell you where to create your working folder for the company data file.

After you have copied the data file to your working folder, rename the file using a unique name. This will help identify your file and reduce the chances of accidentally overwriting a classmate's work. Add your name as an extra footer line on the reports you print. This will further identify your work.

Your instructor will tell you what changes you should make to the filename. You may be asked to add your initials or a code number to the file. For example, you might change **CTB.qbw** to **CTB XX.qbw,** where **XX** represents your initials. Depending on the settings selected in *Microsoft Windows*, the filename extension **.qbw** may or may not display.

Using QuickBooks Pro to Record Transactions

Start *QuickBooks Pro* and open the company data file **CTB XX.qbw** (where **XX** represents your initials or a code number assigned by your instructor). The data file contains the complete chart of accounts. Record the transactions and create the reports under the heading for each month on pages 14–79. Read the following paragraphs for more detailed instructions.

Use the correct date indicated by each transaction. Use the current year in all dates. Key the document number (include *Check* or *Invoice*) or transaction number (include *Transaction*) in the *Memo* field. For adjusting entries, key **Adjusting** in the *Memo* field. For closing entries, key **Closing** in the *Memo* field.

If the *Tracking Fixed Assets* message box appears, check the *Do not display this message in the future* box, and click *No*. You will not create *Fixed Asset Items* in this practice set.

You can print a Trial Balance report (under the *Accountant & Taxes* option of the *Reports* menu) as of March 31, June 30, September 30, and December 31 (before adjusting entries). You can use these Trial Balance reports to compare your *QuickBooks* balances to the check figures on pages 82 and 83. If the *Memorize Report* message box appears when you try to close the report, check the *Do not display this message in the future* box, and click *No*.

After you have completed the last transaction for June (Transaction 19), you are instructed to print a Journal report. The Journal report can be found under the *Accountant & Taxes* option of the *Reports* menu. Use January 1 and June 30 of the current year for the *From* and *To* dates. Change the column widths so that all of the data shows for all columns except *Account*. You may need to allow some account names to be truncated in order to fit the report on one page. Print the report in landscape orientation. If the *Memorize Report* message box appears when you try to close the report, check the *Do not display this message in the future* box, and click *No*. Print other Journal reports as requested in the transactions.

When you view and print the financial statements, use the Profit & Loss Standard report, the Balance Sheet Standard report, and the Statement of Cash Flows report. The Profit & Loss Standard report should be printed before closing entries are made. Remember to add your name on an extra footer line for each report.

You will need to fill out deposit tickets for the checks received in the transactions. (Blank deposit tickets are on pages 84–87.) Fill out one deposit ticket for each work day on which you have one or more checks. Enter all dates using the full month, day, and current year (January 1, 20--). Enter the check number next to the amount.

You will use different windows and features of *QuickBooks* to record the various transactions. The window you should use for each type of transaction is listed below.

1. Use the *Make Deposits* window (from the *Banking* menu) for Transaction 1, Transaction 2, and Transaction 10. Leave the *Received From* field blank, key **Deposit** in the *Memo* field, and choose *Check* from the *Pmt Meth.* drop-down list.

   The checks received in these transactions represent cash receipts that are not payments on account. You will also fill out deposit tickets for the checks in Transactions 1, 2, and 10.

2. Use the *Make General Journal Entries* window (from the *Company* menu) to record transactions that do not involve receipt of cash, cash payments, sales on account, receipts on account, purchases on account, or payments on account.

Transaction 3 (adding Ian Morris as a partner) is an example of an entry that should be recorded in the *General Journal* window. Adjusting and closing entries should also be made in the *General Journal* window.

3. Use the *Write Checks* window (from the *Banking* menu) for cash payments that are not made on account. Make sure that the *Online Payment* and the *To be printed* check boxes are not checked so you can assign check numbers. Begin with Check No. 1101. Number the checks in sequential order for future transactions.

Transaction 4, the rent payment to Dan and Dee Properties, is an example of a transaction for which you should use the *Write Checks* window. Key **Dan and Dee Properties** in the *Pay to the Order of* field. Click in the $ field. If the *Name Not Found* message box appears, click the *Quick Add* button. Click the *Vendor* radio button in the *Select Name Type* dialog box and click *OK*. Dan and Dee Properties is now on the *Vendor List*. Note that for vendors that are created using *Quick Add*, no address will appear on the check.

Once you have used *Quick Add* to set up a vendor, you can choose the vendor from the *Pay to the Order of* drop-down list in future transactions. Repeat this process for all remaining cash payment transactions.

4. Use the *Create Invoices* window (from the *Customers* menu) to invoice for shows or the sale of CDs. If the *Do you want help choosing a sales form?* message box appears, check the *Do not display this message in the future* box, and click *No*. Choose *Intuit Product Invoice* from the *Template* drop-down list. Be sure to enter the correct invoice number.

Select the customer from the *Customer* drop-down list. Enter the quantity sold in the *Quantity* field. Select the correct item from the drop-down list. The *Description* field is filled in by *QuickBooks*. For the *Shows* item, the *Price Each* and the *Amount* fields are completed by *QuickBooks*. For the *CDs* item, you must fill in the *Price Each* field and click in the *Amount* field to calculate *CD Sales* dollars. Repeat the process for all remaining sales to customers.

5. Use the *Receive Payments* window (from the *Customers* menu) to record receipts on account. If the *Merchant Account Service Message* box appears, check the *Do not display this message in the future* box, and click *No*.

Be sure that the *Deposit to* radio button (in the lower-left corner of the window) has been checked and that account *1105 Cash* shows in the box to the right of it. Enter your payment. Repeat the process for all remaining payments received on account.

When a customer makes a payment within the discount period, remember to click the *Set Discount* button. When the *Discount and Credits* dialog box appears, review the discount amount and choose the discount account from the drop-down list. Click *Done* to close the dialog box.

For Transaction 37 (received check from Vallejo Music), you must manually set the sales discount in the *Discount and Credits* dialog box. (Key **20,000.00** in the *Amount of Discount* field.)

6. Use the *Enter Bills* window (under the *Vendors* menu) to record purchases on account. Be sure to use the correct date. Choose the vendor from the drop-down list. The payment terms are automatically entered by *QuickBooks*.

7. Use the *Pay Bills* window (under the *Vendors* menu) to make payments on account. Make sure that the *Assign check no.* radio button is selected. When the *Assign Check Numbers* dialog box appears, click the radio button for *Automatically assign based on next check number for this bank account*. Click *OK* to pay the invoice. This will keep the check numbers in sequence.

Remember to close the company data file after each work session before exiting *QuickBooks*.

Instructions for *Microsoft® Excel* Users

To complete this practice set, you should already have a good working knowledge of *Microsoft® Excel* version 5 or higher. You should also have a good working knowledge of the accounting cycle, including adjusting and closing entries.

The company data file **CTB.xls** is for your use in completing this practice set. This data file can be found in the **CTB** *Excel* folder on the data CD within your textbook. Accounts for the company have been entered in this *Excel* file. The chart of accounts is also shown on page 13 of this textbook.

Copying the Data File

Before you begin recording transactions, you must copy the data file **CTB.xls** to a working folder on a hard drive, a floppy disk, or a network drive so the file can be saved after you edit it. Your instructor will tell you where to create your working folder for the data file.

After you have copied the data file to your working folder, rename the file using a unique name. This will help identify your file and reduce the chances of accidentally overwriting a classmate's work. For every report or ledger page you print, add your name in a footer. This will further identify your work.

Your instructor will tell you what changes you should make to the filename. You may be asked to add your initials or a code number to the file. For example, you might change **CTB.xls** to **CTB XX.xls** where **XX** represents your initials. Depending on the settings selected in *Microsoft Windows*, the filename extension **.xls** may or may not display.

Using the CTB Worksheets

Start *Excel* and open the renamed data file **CTB XX.xls** from your working folder. Record the transactions and create the reports under the heading for each month on pages 14–79. Read the paragraphs below for more detailed instructions on using the worksheets.

The CTB workbook (data file) contains nine worksheets. Each sheet should be used for the purposes described below.

1. The *General Ledger* sheet should be used to record all journal entries. All debits should be entered as positive numbers. All credits should be entered as negative numbers. (Place a minus symbol in front of the number.)

One journal entry should be made in each column for Transactions 1 through 61. All adjusting entries should be made in one column. All closing entries should be made in one column. Be sure to use the correct column for each transaction. Enter the date of the transaction in the cell above *Transaction* for each transaction. For the date, use this format: 1/3/20--. Use the current year in dates.

Some transactions may require more than one entry to an account. In these instances, the individual entries to an account should be added together and put in the *General Ledger* column for that transaction number. For example, suppose each partner withdraws $10,000.00 from the business. Each partner's drawing account would be debited for $10,000.00. The Cash account would be credited for the combined amount, $50,000.00.

Compare the *Account Balance Before Adjustments* column to the check figures on pages 82 and 83 after you have completed the transactions for March, June, September, and December (before making the adjusting entries).

2. The *Invoices* sheet contains the blank forms you will use to create invoices for transactions in which CTB needs to bill a customer (for live performances or the sale of CDs). Be sure to use the correct date, customer name and address, and payment terms on each invoice. Check unit and dollar amounts to make sure they are correct. Enter all dates using the full month, day, and current year (January 1, 20--).

An entry should be made on the *General Journal* sheet to debit Accounts Receivable and credit the appropriate sales account to record each invoice. An entry should also be posted to the customer account on the *Acc. Rec. Ledger*.

3. The *Acc. Rec. Ledger* sheet should be used to record changes in a specific customer account as a result of an invoice or a cash receipt. Each sale or cash receipt on account transaction should also be recorded on the *General Ledger* sheet.

Enter all dates using the full month, day, and current year (January 1, 20--). Credit amounts should be recorded in the credit column as positive amounts (no minus sign). If the sale or cash receipt on account is recorded correctly, the *Total Accounts Receivable* in cell E67 should equal the total for *Accounts Receivable* in cell BL9 on the *General Ledger* sheet.

4. The *Acc. Pay. Ledger* sheet should be used to record changes in a specific vendor account as a result of a purchase or a cash payment on account. Each purchase or cash payment on account transaction should also be recorded on the *General Ledger* sheet.

   Enter all dates using the full month, day, and current year (January 1, 20--). Credit amounts should be recorded in the credit column as positive amounts (no minus sign). If the purchase or cash payment on account is recorded correctly, the *Total Accounts Payable* in cell E22 should equal the total for *Accounts Payable* in cell BL22 on the *General Ledger* sheet.

5. The *Checks* sheet contains blank checks and the check register (on the check stubs) for CTB. A check should be written for each payment transaction. The *Date, To, For*, and *Amount* on the check register will be completed automatically by *Excel* using the information you enter on the check. Enter all dates using the full month, day, and current year (January 1, 20--). You may apply a signature to the checks, but it is not necessary for this simulation.

   Be sure to review each check carefully. Each time you create a check, you need to credit Cash and debit the appropriate account on the *General Ledger* sheet.

   For each day with transactions in which you have a check, you should fill out a deposit ticket. (Blank deposit tickets are on pages 84–87.) Enter all dates using the full month, day, and current year (January 1, 20--). Enter the check number next to the amount.

   Each deposit ticket should be recorded on the appropriate line of the stub of the next blank check. If more than one deposit is received since you wrote the last check, record the deposits on the same check stub. Adjustments to cash (interest income) should also be recorded on the next blank check stub.

   If the check, deposit, adjustment, and the *General Ledger* transaction are correct, the *Balance Forward* on the stub of the next blank check should equal cell BL8 on the *General Ledger* sheet.

6. The *Income Statement, Balance Sheet, Owner's Equity*, and *Cash Flows* sheets each contain a report. The data are filled in by *Excel*, based on the transactions you enter on the *General Ledger* sheet. When you finish all of the transactions, adjusting entries, and closing entries, add a custom footer that includes your name to each report and print it.

The table below is a summary of the transactions that go on each sheet.

SHEET	TRANSACTION TYPE
General Ledger	All transactions, adjusting entries, and closing entries
Invoices	All sales on account
Acc. Rec. Ledger	All sales and cash receipts on account
Acc. Pay. Ledger	All purchases and cash payments on account
Checks	All payments, deposits, and adjustments to cash
Income Statement	Calculated by Excel
Balance Sheet	Calculated by Excel
Owner's Equity	Calculated by Excel
Cash Flows	Calculated by Excel

When using the **CTB XX.xls** file, do not insert or delete rows or columns. Do not move data to a different row or column. Deleting or moving data will cause errors in the sheets that contain reports (*Balance Sheet, Income Statement, Owner's Equity,* and *Cash Flows*).

Remember to save the data file after each work session before exiting *Excel.*

Chart of Accounts

Account No.	Account	Account No.	Account
	Current Assets		**Sales**
1105	Cash	4105	CD Sales
1107	Accounts Receivable	4110	CD Sales Discount
1115	Inventory	4115	Club Show Income
1120	Prepaid Deposits		**Cost of Goods Sold**
1125	Prepaid Expenses	5102	Beginning Inventory
	Plant Assets	5105	Purchases
1205	Computer Equipment	5110	Purchases Discount
1210	Acc. Depr.—Comp. Equipment	5115	Ending Inventory
1215	Office Furniture		**Expenses**
1220	Acc. Depr.—Office Furniture	6105	Advertising Expense
	Other Assets	6110	Amortization Expense
1305	Capitalized Studio Costs	6115	Depr. Exp.—Computer Equipment
1310	Goodwill	6120	Depr. Exp.—Office Furniture
	Current Liabilities	6125	Donations Expense
2105	Accounts Payable	6130	Employer Payroll Taxes Expense
2110	Employer Taxes Payable	6135	Office Workers Expense
2115	Employee Income Taxes Payable	6140	Rent Expense
2120	Unearned Rent	6145	Salary Expense
	Long-Term Liability	6150	Security Expense
2205	Loan Payable	6155	Supplies Expense
	Owner's Equity	6160	Utilities Expense
3105	Kyle Jaffe, Capital		**Other Income**
3110	Kyle Jaffe, Drawing	7105	Rent Income
3115	Kacy Jaffe, Capital	7110	Interest Income
3120	Kacy Jaffe, Drawing		**Other Expense**
3125	Bernadette Yap, Capital	8105	Interest Expense
3130	Bernadette Yap, Drawing		
3135	Joey Yap, Capital		
3140	Joey Yap, Drawing		
3145	Ian Morris, Capital		
3150	Ian Morris, Drawing		
3195	Income Summary		

In *QuickBooks*, use the
Make Deposits window.

In *Peachtree*, use the
General Journal Entry
window.

In *Excel*, use the *General
Ledger* sheet.

January Transactions

Transactions 1 and 2 will establish working funds for the business.

Transaction 1 ▶ January 3

Record the transaction for deposit of a check for $80,000.00, representing a
$20,000.00 capital contribution by each of the four band members: Kyle Jaffe,
Kacy Jaffe, Joey Yap, and Bernadette Yap. (Debit Cash and credit the capital
account for each band member.)

Begin a deposit ticket for January 3 transactions. Deposit tickets are found on
pages 84–87. Enter the check for $80,000.00 on the deposit ticket. (Do not
total the deposit ticket. More checks will be added later.) Remember to enter
the check number by the check amount on the deposit ticket.

cashier's check: check issued by a bank on its own
account for the amount paid to the bank by the purchaser

Transaction 2 ▶ January 3

Record the transaction for deposit of a check for $12,000.00 received from a
loan payable. The money comes from a loan from Kyle and Kacy Jaffe's parents ($6,000.00) and from Joey and Bernadette Yap's parents ($6,000.00).
Record the transaction as one loan payable. The money will be used to pay
the rent and utilities on the band's practice and storage space for one year.
(Debit Cash and credit Loan Payable.)

Add this check to the deposit ticket begun for January 3 transactions. Total
the deposit ticket.

	$\frac{29\text{-}787}{719}$ 000002006
CASHIER'S CHECK	**Pay to the order of** **Date** January 3, 20--
	CTB --- $ 12,000.00
	Amount $12,000 AND NO CENTS
	Authorized Signature *Roberto A. Perez*
	(For Classroom Use Only)
	★**All Star Bank** Crystal Lake, IL 60014

Transaction 3 ▶ January 3

Ian Morris, a long-time friend, has suggested making a music video of one of the band's original songs. The band members agreed to make the video with Ian. Ian will supervise and pay production costs for the music video. He will also become the band's videographer and agent.

The band members agree that Ian's contribution of creating the music video and his expertise in the music business are valued at $20,000.00. Ian will be an equal partner in the business and will share equally in future earnings.

Record the transaction to make Ian Morris a partner. (Debit Goodwill and credit Ian Morris, Capital for $20,000.00.) To learn more about goodwill, read the FYI below.

intangible asset: an asset that has value for a business but does not exist physically; examples include patents, copyrights, trademarks, and goodwill

Goodwill

Goodwill is a form of **intangible asset** that is created from the value added to a business as a result of favorable location, good reputation, or managerial ability. In our example, the band members feel that Ian Morris's contribution of creating the music video and his expertise in the music business are worth $20,000.

Transaction 4 ▶ January 12

Pay the invoice for rent for the space the band is renting. The rental agreement calls for the rent to be paid for one year in advance. (Debit Prepaid Expenses.)

Dan and Dee Properties
1235 Rance Road
Algonquin, IL 60102-0256

Invoice No.: 111334

To:

CTB
2244 Brian Avenue
Crystal Lake, IL 60014-0065

Invoice Date: January 5, 20--

Item	Quantity	Amount	Total
Rent for studio space (monthly)	12	$700.00	$8,400.00

Due Date	January 15, 20--		Total Due	$8,400.00

Pay the invoice for $100.00 for hooking up electricity at the studio. The invoice includes a $50.00 connection fee and a $50.00 deposit. The invoice is accompanied by a note to the accountant to write a check to Local Electric, Inc., for $2,400.00. The band thinks this amount will cover the expense for the entire year. (Debit Prepaid Expenses for $2,350.00 and Prepaid Deposits for $50.00.)

		Invoice No.:	17765
		Invoice Date:	January 5, 20--

Local Electric, Inc.
17540 Dominick Lane
Chicago, IL 60654-1750

Account Number	Account Name	Service Address	Meter Number
20072602	CTB	2244 Brian Avenue Crystal Lake, IL 60014-0065	32955

Service	Amount
Deposit for new account	$ 50.00
Connection fee	50.00

Date Due	February 10, 20--	**Total Due**	$100.00

January 12

Write the check to Local Electric, Inc., for $2,400.00. This amount should cover the expense for the entire year.

Kacy

Transaction 6 ▶ January 12

Pay the invoice for $100.00 to have a telephone connected at the studio. The invoice includes a $50.00 connection fee and a $50.00 deposit. A note to the accountant accompanies the invoice. Write the check for $1,200.00 to cover what the band thinks will be the expense for the entire year. (Debit Prepaid Expenses for $1,150.00 and Prepaid Deposits for $50.00.)

RAMIZ Telephone
6658 Nino Drive
Harvard, IL 60033-0660

Invoice No.: 55577

To:
CTB
2244 Brian Avenue
Crystal Lake, IL 60014-0065

Invoice Date: January 5, 20--

Item	Amount	Total
Connection Fee	$50.00	$ 50.00
Deposit	50.00	50.00

Due Date	February 10, 20--	Total Due	$100.00

January 12

Write the check to Ramiz Telephone for $1,200.00. This amount should cover the expense for the entire year.

Kacy

Pay the invoice from an office furniture store for purchase of office furniture that will be used by the band.

			Invoice No.:	39629

Bell's Office Furniture
2112 Rush Street
Chicago, IL 60622-2112

To: **Invoice Date:** January 8, 20--

CTB
2244 Brian Avenue
Crystal Lake, IL 60014-0065

Item	Quantity	Amount	Total
Office Desk #45826	2	$1,200.00	$2,400.00
Due Date February 8, 20--		**Total Due**	$2,400.00

Transaction 8 ▶ January 12

Pay the invoice for computer equipment and office supplies. Debit the amount and applicable sales tax for the computer, cable, surge suppressor, and printer to Computer Equipment. Debit the amount and applicable sales tax for the other items to Supplies Expense.

Jefferson Office Supply
143 St. Charles Place
Chicago, IL 60612

To:
CTB
2244 Brian Avenue
Crystal Lake, IL 60014-0065

Invoice Date: January 8, 20--
Invoice No.: 5223417

Quantity	Description	Unit Price	Amount
1	Formatted diskettes, 100 pack	$25.00	$ 25.00
1	CD-R, 50 pack	24.95	24.95
5	Pens, black fine point, 5 pack	3.95	19.75
10	Legal pads, yellow, 3 pack	2.55	25.50
5	Envelopes, No. 10, 100 per box	6.35	31.75
1	Stapler with staples	5.00	5.00
1	Paper, 8 1/2 x 11, 12 reams	35.00	35.00
1	Note pads, sticky back, 12 pack	6.00	6.00
1	Notebook computer	2,155.95	2,155.95
1	USB cable for printer	12.99	12.99
1	Surge suppressor strip	19.99	19.99
1	Printer, color laser	2,344.00	2,344.00
	Sales Tax (6.25%)		294.12

Due Date	February 10, 20--	**Total Due**	$5,000.00

February Transactions

On February 5, the band contracted with a recording studio for 240 hours of studio time at $185 per hour. Half of the fee is payable now. The other half is due upon completion of recording.

Transaction 9 ▶ February 10

Pay the invoice for studio recording time. Record the cost for the studio recording time as an asset. (Debit Capitalized Studio Costs.) To learn more about recording and amortizing intangible assets, read the FYI on the next page.

Invoice No.:	223971			

ASF Recording Solutions
5521 Bella Avenue
Chicago, IL 60625-5521

Invoice Date: February 4, 20--

To:
CTB
2244 Brian Avenue
Crystal Lake, IL 60014-0065

Quantity	Description	Unit Price	Amount
120	Studio rental, hourly	$185.00	$22,200.00
		Total Due	$22,200.00

Amortization

The purchase of a service (such as recording time in a studio) is usually recorded as an expense. When the service will benefit the company for an extended period of time (more than one year), however, the service is sometimes recorded as an asset. Recording the cost of a service as an asset is called *capitalizing* the service. A capitalized service is a form of intangible asset.

Amortization is a method of gradually expensing the cost of intangible assets over a period of time. The time period varies according to the type of intangible asset. For example, patents on inventions are usually valid for 20 years. However, the costs associated with a patent can be amortized over a shorter period if management thinks that the useful life of the asset will be shorter.

In this practice set, the band members think that the **useful life** of the Capitalized Studio Costs is until the end of next year. They also think that half of the cost should be expensed this year and half next year.

useful life: the period of time during which a fixed asset or intangible asset has value to a business

March Transactions

Transaction 10 ▶ March 10

sublet: to rent property (to another party) that you yourself have rented

Software Tip

In *Excel*, record the deposit ticket total on the *Checks* sheet.

CTB has agreed to **sublet** their practice studio to another band for two nights per week for one year. The rental amount is $1,200.00 for the year, to be paid in advance. Record the transaction for deposit of the check from Park & Yung, Inc., for studio rental. (Credit Unearned Rent.)

Begin a deposit ticket for March 10 transactions. Deposit tickets are found on pages 84–87. Enter the check for $1,200.00 on the deposit ticket. Total the deposit ticket.

Park & Yung, Inc.
555 Koehler Drive
Ingelside, IL 60041-0555

No. 3978   29-787 / 719

Date March 1, 20--

PAY TO THE ORDER OF CTB --- $ 1,200.00

One thousand two hundred and 00/100-------------- **Dollars**

All Star Bank
Crystal Lake, IL 60014

MEMO Studio Rental

Kim Park

(For Classroom Use Only)

Transaction 11 ▶ March 10

Pay the invoice for the final amount to the recording studio. The invoice total should be recorded as Capitalized Studio Costs.

Invoice No.:   223985

ASF Recording Solutions
5521 Bella Avenue
Chicago, IL 60625-5521

Invoice Date: March 7, 20--

To:

CTB
2244 Brian Avenue
Crystal Lake, IL 60014-0065

Quantity	Description	Unit Price	Amount
130	Studio rental, hourly	$ 185.00	$24,500.00
1	CD remaster	2,000.00	2,000.00
		Total Due	$26,500.00

Transaction 12 ► March 31

A reproduction company produced 10,000 CDs of the band's recording from the master created in the studio. Pay the invoice for reproduction of CDs. (Debit Purchases and credit Cash.)

HABIB DUPLICATING
4422 Jackson Blvd.
Buffalo Grove, IL 60089-4422

Invoice No.: 33078

To:
CTB
2244 Brian Avenue
Crystal Lake, IL 60014-0065

Invoice Date: March 25, 20--
Terms: Net 30

Quantity	Description	Unit Price	Amount
10,000	Music CD with sleeve	2.25	$22,500.00
		Total Due	$22,500.00

Transaction 13 ▶ March 31

The band has played at Club Low every Friday night for the first quarter of the year. (Assume there are 13 Fridays in the first quarter.) Create an invoice to Club Low. Use March 31 for the date. Use Invoice No. 1000. The club's address is:

Club Low
12446 Virginia Road
Crystal Lake, IL 60014-0446

The band is billing for 13 shows at $400.00 per show. Also, the band sold to Club Low 5,000 CDs at $4.00 each. The club will resell the CDs to patrons (so there is no sales tax for this invoice). The terms for the invoice are Net 30. Debit Club Low, Accounts Receivable for the invoice total. Credit Club Show Income for the shows and CD Sales for the sale of CDs.

Accounting Tip

After completing the March transactions, compare your account balances to the check figures for January through March on pages 82 and 83.

Transaction 14 ▶ March 31

The band has played at The Leading Edge every Saturday night for the first quarter of the year. (Assume there are 13 Saturdays in the first quarter.) Create an invoice to The Leading Edge. Use March 31 for the date. Use Invoice No. 1001. The club's address is:

The Leading Edge
1078 Virginia Road
Crystal Lake, IL 60014-1078

The band is billing for 13 shows at $400.00 per show. Also, the band sold to The Leading Edge 5,000 CDs at $4.00 each. The club will resell the CDs to patrons (so there is no sales tax for this invoice). The terms for the invoice are Net 30.

April Transactions

Transaction 15 ▶ April 12

Pay the invoice from the accountant (you) for work for the band for the first quarter of the current year. (Debit Office Workers Expense.)

Student Name
8725 Dee Way
Palatine, IL 60038-0752

Invoice No.: 4401

To:
CTB
2244 Brian Avenue
Crystal Lake, IL 60014-0065

Invoice Date: April 10, 20--
Terms: Net 10

Quantity	Description	Unit Price	Amount
35	Accounting services, hourly January through March 20--	$30.00	$1,050.00
		Total Due	$1,050.00

Transaction 16 ▶ April 12

Record the transaction for deposit of the check received from Club Low for Invoice No. 1000. (Debit Cash and credit Club Low, Accounts Receivable.)

Begin a deposit ticket for April 12 transactions. Deposit tickets are found on pages 84–87. Enter the check for $25,200.00 on the deposit ticket. (Do not total the deposit ticket. More checks will be added later.)

Club Low
12446 Virginia Road
Crystal Lake, IL 60041-0446

No. 4355   29-787
               719

Date April 6, 20--

PAY TO THE
ORDER OF CTB --- $ 25,200.00

Twenty-five thousand two hundred and 00/100 --- **Dollars**

☆**All Star Bank**
   Crystal Lake, IL 60014

MEMO Shows and CDs

Joey Chin

(For Classroom Use Only)

Transaction 17 ▶ April 12

Record the transaction for deposit of a check received from The Leading Edge for Invoice No. 1001. (Debit Cash and credit The Leading Edge, Accounts Receivable.)

Continue completing the deposit ticket for April 12 transactions. Enter the check for $25,200.00 on the deposit ticket. Total the deposit ticket.

The Leading Edge
1078 Virginia Road
Crystal Lake, IL 60014-1078

No. 4134   29-787 / 719

Date _April 8, 20--_

PAY TO THE ORDER OF _CTB_ -- $ 25,200.00

Twenty-five thousand two hundred and 00/100 --- **Dollars**

All Star Bank
Crystal Lake, IL 60014

MEMO _Shows and CDs_

Maria Gomez
(For Classroom Use Only)

June Transactions

Transaction 18 ▶ June 30

The band has played at Club Low every Friday night for the second quarter of the year. Create an invoice to Club Low. Use June 30 for the date. Use Invoice No. 1002. The club's address is:

Club Low
12446 Virginia Road
Crystal Lake, IL 60014-0446

The band is billing for 13 shows at $400.00 per show. The terms for the invoice are Net 30.

Accounting Tip

After completing the June transactions, compare your account balances to the check figures for April through June on pages 82 and 83.

Transaction 19 ▶ June 30

The band has played at The Leading Edge every Saturday night for the second quarter of the year. Create an invoice to The Leading Edge. Use June 30 for the date. Use Invoice No. 1003. The club's address is:

The Leading Edge
1078 Virginia Road
Crystal Lake, IL 60014-1078

The band is billing for 13 shows at $400.00 per show. The terms for the invoice are Net 30.

Print a Report ▶ June 30

After you have completed all of the transactions for January through June, print a report showing transactions for January 1 through June 30, 20--.

Peachtree users: Print a General Ledger report.

QuickBooks users: Print a Journal report. Add your name in a footer on the report.

Excel users: Print the *General Ledger* sheet showing columns A and B and transactions for January through June. Add your name in a footer on the sheet.

July Transactions

The band's music video is getting a large amount of airplay on several music TV channels. Music CDs by CTB are in demand. In the past, some CDs were produced and sold at clubs where the band plays. Now the band must greatly increase production of CDs.

Transaction 20 ▶ July 10

A reproduction company produced 150,000 CDs of the band's recording from the master created in the studio. Do not pay the invoice at this time. Debit Purchases and credit Habib Duplicating, Accounts Payable.

● HABIB DUPLICATING	4422 Jackson Blvd. Buffalo Grove, IL 60089-4422		Invoice No.:	34297

To:
CTB
2244 Brian Avenue
Crystal Lake, IL 60014-0065

Invoice Date: July 8, 20--
Terms: Net 30

Quantity	Description	Unit Price	Amount
150,000	Music CD with sleeve	$1.50	$225,000.00
		Total Due	$225,000.00

Pay the invoice from the accountant (you) for work for the band for the second quarter of the current year.

			Invoice No.:	4402

Student Name
8725 Dee Way
Palatine, IL 60038-0752

To:
    CTB
    2244 Brian Avenue
    Crystal Lake, IL 60014-0065

Invoice Date: July 1, 20--
Terms: Net 10

Quantity	Description	Unit Price	Amount
40	Accounting services, hourly April through June 20--	$30.00	$1,200.00
		Total Due	$1,200.00

Transaction 22 ▶ July 10

Record the transaction for deposit of a check received from Club Low for Invoice No. 1002.

Begin a deposit ticket for July 10 transactions. Deposit tickets are found on pages 84–87. Enter the check for $5,200.00 on the deposit ticket. (Do not total the deposit ticket. More checks will be added later.)

Club Low
12446 Virginia Road
Crystal Lake, IL 60041-0446

No. 4422   29-787
             719

Date July 6, 20--

PAY TO THE
ORDER OF CTB -- $ 5,200.00

Five thousand two hundred and 00/100 ------------- **Dollars**

All Star Bank
Crystal Lake, IL 60014

MEMO Shows

Joey Chin

(For Classroom Use Only)

Transaction 23 ▶ July 10

Record the transaction for deposit of a check received from The Leading Edge for Invoice No. 1003.

Continue completing the deposit ticket for July 10 transactions. Enter the check for $5,200.00 on the deposit ticket. Total the deposit ticket.

The Leading Edge
1078 Virginia Road
Crystal Lake, IL 60014-1078

No. 4677

29-787
719

Date April 8, 20--

PAY TO THE
ORDER OF CTB --- $ 5,200.00

Five thousand two hundred and 00/100 ------------- Dollars

All Star Bank
Crystal Lake, IL 60014

MEMO Shows

Maria Gomez

(For Classroom Use Only)

Transaction 24 ▶ July 28

Create an invoice to Distributors, Inc., for the sale of CDs. Use July 28 for the date. Use Invoice No. 1004. The address is:

Distributors, Inc.
2200 Palms Way
Boca Raton, FL 33428-2200

The band is billing for 75,000 CDs at $8.00 each. The terms for the invoice are 2/10 Net 30.

A reproduction company produced 150,000 CDs of the band's recording from the master created in the studio. Do not pay the invoice at this time. Debit Purchases and credit Mahan Recording, Accounts Payable.

		Invoice No.: 77752
Mahan Recording 7710 Mountain Road Elgin, IL 60120-7710		
To: CTB 2244 Brian Avenue Crystal Lake, IL 60014-0065		**Invoice Date:** July 20, 20-- **Terms:** Net 30

Quantity	Description	Unit Price	Amount
150,000	Music CD with sleeve	$1.50	$225,000.00
		Total Due	$225,000.00

Transaction 26 ▶ July 28

Pay the invoice for telephone charges. A note accompanies the invoice instructing you to write the check for $1,500.00 to cover what the band thinks will be the expense for the remainder of the year. (Debit Prepaid Expenses.)

RAMIZ Telephone
6658 Nino Drive
Harvard, IL 60033-0660

Invoice No.: 62460

To:
CTB
2244 Brian Avenue
Crystal Lake, IL 60014-0065

Invoice Date: July 25, 20--

Item	Amount	Total
Previous Balance	($300.00)	($300.00)
Current Month Charges	400.00	400.00

Due Date	August 10, 20--	**Total Due**	$100.00

July 28

Write the check for $1,500.00.
This should cover the expense
for the remainder of the year.

Kacy

August Transactions

The band is becoming quite successful. Because of its increasing success, CTB hired two office workers at the beginning of July. The workers are from a temporary service. The band plans to hire them permanently if they do a good job. The primary responsibilities of the temporary workers are to:

◆ Sort and open incoming mail

◆ Answer the telephones and either transfer the calls or take messages

◆ Process outgoing mail

◆ Handle the receipt and shipment of CDs (the accountant will handle all transactions)

◆ Make travel arrangements for the band and manager

◆ Answer inquires regarding bookings for the band

◆ Help create publicity materials

Transaction 27 ▶ August 5

Pay the July invoice for the temporary workers. (Debit Office Workers Expense and credit Cash.)

Cortez Staffing Solutions
7753 Alan Road
Lake in the Hills, IL 60156-7753

Invoice No.: 3765
Invoice Date: August 1, 20--

To:
CTB
2244 Brian Avenue
Crystal Lake, IL 60014-0065

Terms: Net 10

Quantity	Description	Unit Price	Amount
160	Yolanda Winfrey, hours worked in July	$25.00	$4,000.00
160	Saray Ponnas, hours worked in July	25.00	4,000.00
		Total Due	$8,000.00

Transaction 28 ▶ August 5

Create an invoice to Recorded Music Distributors for the sale of CDs. Use August 5 for the date. Use Invoice No. 1005. The address is:

Recorded Music Distributors
8801 Creek Court
Palatine, IL 60038-8801

The band is billing for 120,000 CDs at $10.00 each. The terms for the invoice are 2/10 Net 30.

Record the transaction for deposit of a check received from Distributors, Inc., for Invoice No. 1004, less 2% discount.

Complete a deposit ticket for August 5 transactions. Deposit tickets are found on pages 84–87. Enter the check for $588,000.00 on the deposit ticket. Total the deposit ticket.

Distributors, Inc.	No. 1433 92-788 / 631
2200 Palms Way	
Boca Raton, FL 33428-2200	
	Date August 2, 20--
PAY TO THE ORDER OF CTB ---	$ 588,000.00
Five hundred eighty-eight thousand and 00/100 --- **Dollars**	
BOCA Bank & Trust	
Boca Raton, FL 33428	
MEMO Invoice 1004 less discount	*Jonathan Sanchez*
	FOR CLASSROOM USE ONLY

Issue a check for $6,000.00 to Ian Morris to reimburse travel expenses.

MEMORANDUM

TO: Student Name

FROM: Ian Morris

DATE: August 5, 20--

SUBJECT: Expense Reimbursement

Please reimburse me for $6,000.00 of expenses I charged to my credit card. The expenses were incurred on our publicity trip to New York. Charge the expenses to Advertising Expense.

Thanks.

Issue a check to each partner for $25,000.00. Record the transaction for this draw from capital.

MEMORANDUM

TO: Student Name

FROM: Kacy Jaffe

DATE: August 5, 20--

SUBJECT: Payment of Profits

Please pay each partner (band members and manager) $25,000.00 each. The amount should be recorded as a draw from each capital account.

Thanks.

Issue checks to pay vendors on account.

MEMORANDUM

TO: Student Name

FROM: Kacy Jaffe

DATE: August 5, 20--

SUBJECT: Payments to Vendors

Please pay Habib Duplicating and Mahan Recording the balances we owe them. Please remember to indicate the invoice numbers on the checks.

Thanks.

Transaction 33 ▸ August 15

Create an invoice to Vallejo Music, Inc., for the sale of CDs. Use August 15 for the date. Use Invoice No. 1006. The address is:

Vallejo Music, Inc.
8834 Trail Road
Vallejo, CA 94591-8834

The band is billing for 100,000 CDs at $10.00 each. The terms for the invoice are 2/10 Net 30.

Transaction 34 ▶ August 15

Record the transaction for deposit of a check received from Recorded Music Distributors for Invoice No. 1005.

Complete a deposit ticket for August 15 transactions. Deposit tickets are found on pages 84–87. Enter the check for $1,176,000.00 on the deposit ticket. Total the deposit ticket.

Recorded Music Distributors
8801 Creek Court
Palatine, IL 60038-8801

No. 4334   71-924
            ———
            277

Date August 13, 20--

PAY TO THE
ORDER OF CTB --- $ 1,176,000.00

One million one hundred seventy-six thousand and 00/100 **Dollars**

Palatine
BANK & TRUST
Palatine, IL 60038

MEMO Invoice 1005 less discount

Frances Graves

(For Classroom Use Only)

Because of CTB's increasing popularity, the band needs to hire security for their live performances. CTB is contracted to do 13 more shows for Club Low and 13 more shows for The Leading Edge. The band will receive $400.00 for each show. Even though the cost for security is more than CTB receives for the live performances, it is necessary to protect the band members and their equipment. (Debit Security Expense.)

Invoice No.: 7964
Invoice Date: August 10, 20--

Southwood Security
2828 N. Michigan Avenue
Chicago, IL 60612-2828

To:

CTB
2244 Brian Avenue
Crystal Lake, IL 60014-0065

Terms: Net 30

Quantity	Description	Unit Price	Amount
26	Provide security for live shows	$1,000.00	$26,000.00
		Total Due	$26,000.00

Pay off the loan from the band members' parents. The loan is for $12,000.00 plus interest.

MEMORANDUM

TO: Student Name

FROM: Kacy Jaffe

DATE: August 15, 20--

SUBJECT: Payment of Loan

Please pay off the loan from the band members' parents. Pay Sally and Morris Jaffe $6,375.00 ($6,000.00 principal and $375.00 interest). Pay Margaret and Joseph Yap $6,375.00 ($6,000.00 principal and $375.00 interest).

Thanks.

Transaction 37 ▶ August 30

Record the transaction for deposit of a check received from Vallejo Music, Inc., on August 25 for Invoice No. 1006.

Complete a deposit ticket for August 30 transactions. Deposit tickets are found on pages 84–87. Enter the check for $980,000.00 on the deposit ticket. Total the deposit ticket.

Vallejo Music, Inc.
8834 Trail Road
Vallejo, CA 94591-8834

No. 7668   12-114
                522

Date August 23, 20--

PAY TO THE
ORDER OF   CTB -- $ 980,000.00

Nine hundred eighty thousand and 00/100 --------------------- **Dollars**

VALLEJO
Bank & Trust
Vallejo, CA 94591

MEMO Invoice 1006 less discount

Juliana Santos
(For Classroom Use Only)

September Transactions

Pay the invoice for the temporary workers.

Cortez Staffing Solutions
7753 Alan Road
Lake in the Hills, IL 60156-7753

Invoice No.: 3826
Invoice Date: September 1, 20--

To:
CTB
2244 Brian Avenue
Crystal Lake, IL 60014-0065

Terms: Net 10

Quantity	Description	Unit Price	Amount
160	Yolanda Winfrey, hours worked in August	$25.00	$4,000.00
160	Saray Ponnas, hours worked in August	25.00	4,000.00
		Total Due	$8,000.00

A reproduction company produced 300,000 CDs of the band's recording from the master created in the studio. Pay the invoice now and take the discount.

HABIB DUPLICATING 4422 Jackson Blvd. Buffalo Grove, IL 60089-4422	**Invoice No.:** 35664

To:
CTB
2244 Brian Avenue
Crystal Lake, IL 60014-0065

Invoice Date: September 1, 20--
Terms: 2/10, n/30

Quantity	Description	Unit Price	Amount
300,000	Music CD with sleeve	$1.25	$375,000.00
		Total Due	$375,000.00

The band has played at Club Low every Friday night for the third quarter of the year. Create an invoice to Club Low. Use September 30 for the date. Use Invoice No. 1007. The club's address is:

Club Low
12446 Virginia Road
Crystal Lake, IL 60014-0446

The band is billing for 13 shows at $400.00 per show. The terms for the invoice are Net 30.

Transaction 41 ▶ September 30

The band has played at The Leading Edge every Saturday night for the third quarter of the year. Create an invoice to The Leading Edge. Use September 30 for the date. Use Invoice No. 1008. The club's address is:

The Leading Edge
1078 Virginia Road
Crystal Lake, IL 60014-1078

The band is billing for 13 shows at $400.00 per show. The terms for the invoice are Net 30.

October Transactions

Pay the invoice for the temporary workers.

Cortez Staffing Solutions
7753 Alan Road
Lake in the Hills, IL 60156-7753

Invoice No.: 3898
Invoice Date: October 1, 20--

To:

    CTB
    2244 Brian Avenue
    Crystal Lake, IL 60014-0065

Terms: Net 10

Quantity	Description	Unit Price	Amount
160	Yolanda Winfrey, hours worked in September	$25.00	$4,000.00
160	Saray Ponnas, hours worked in September	25.00	4,000.00
		Total Due	$8,000.00

Transaction 43 ▶ October 10

Pay the invoice from the accountant (you) for work for the band for the third quarter of the current year.

Student Name
8725 Dee Way
Palatine, IL 60038-0752

Invoice No.: 4403

To:
CTB
2244 Brian Avenue
Crystal Lake, IL 60014-0065

Invoice Date: October 10, 20--
Terms: Net 10

Quantity	Description	Unit Price	Amount
220	Accounting services, hourly July through September 20--	$30.00	$6,600.00
		Total Due	$6,600.00

Transaction 44 ▶ October 10

Record the transaction for deposit of a check received from Club Low for Invoice No. 1007.

Begin a deposit ticket for October 10 transactions. Deposit tickets are found on pages 84–87. Enter the check for $5,200.00 on the deposit ticket. (Do not total the deposit ticket. More checks will be added later.)

Club Low		No. 4650	29-787 / 719
12446 Virginia Road			
Crystal Lake, IL 60041-0446			

Date October 6, 20--

PAY TO THE
ORDER OF   CTB --- $ 5,200.00

Five thousand two hundred and 00/100 ------------- Dollars

All Star Bank
Crystal Lake, IL 60014

MEMO Shows

Joey Chin

(For Classroom Use Only)

Transaction 45 ▶ October 10

Record the transaction for deposit of the check received from The Leading Edge for Invoice No. 1008.

Continue completing the deposit ticket for October 10 transactions. Enter the check for $5,200.00 on the deposit ticket. Total the deposit ticket.

The Leading Edge
1078 Virginia Road
Crystal Lake, IL 60014-1078

No. 4801   29-787 / 719

Date October 8, 20--

PAY TO THE
ORDER OF CTB -- $ 5,200.00

Five thousand two hundred and 00/100 ------------- **Dollars**

★All Star Bank
Crystal Lake, IL 60014

MEMO Shows

Maria Gomez
(For Classroom Use Only)

Transaction 46 ▶ October 31

Create an invoice to Distributors, Inc., for the sale of CDs. Use October 31 for the date. Use Invoice No. 1009. The address is:

Distributors, Inc.
2200 Palms Way
Boca Raton, FL 33428-2200

The band is billing for 75,000 CDs at $10.00 each. The terms for the invoice are 2/10 Net 30.

Transaction 47 ▶ October 31

Create an invoice to Recorded Music Distributors for the sale of CDs. Use October 31 for the date. Use Invoice No. 1010. The address is:

Recorded Music Distributors
8801 Creek Court
Palatine, IL 60038-8801

The band is billing for 75,000 CDs at $10.00 each. The terms for the invoice are 2/10 Net 30.

Transaction 48 ▶ October 31

Issue a check for $15,000.00 to Ian Morris to reimburse travel expenses. (Debit Advertising Expense.)

MEMORANDUM

TO: Student Name

FROM: Ian Morris

DATE: October 31, 20--

SUBJECT: Expense Reimbursement

Please reimburse me for $15,000.00 of expenses I charged to my credit card. The expenses were incurred on our recent publicity trip.

Thanks.

November Transactions

The partners are very satisfied with the work you, Yolanda Winfrey, and Saray Ponnas have been doing. They made a decision to employ the three of you full time as of November 1, 20--.

The payroll will be calculated and the checks will be issued by Duncan Payroll Services. You will receive a summary payroll report. You will write a check to fund the net payroll and a check to pay the payroll tax liability. Both of the checks will be written to Duncan Payroll Services. The company will send a courier to pick up the checks.

Transaction 49 ▶ November 10

Record the transaction for deposit of the check received from Distributors, Inc., for Invoice No. 1009.

Begin a deposit ticket for November 10 transactions. Deposit tickets are found on pages 84–87. Enter the check for $735,000.00 on the deposit ticket. (Do not total the deposit ticket. More checks will be added later.)

Distributors, Inc.	No. 1627 92-788
2200 Palms Way	631
Boca Raton, FL 33428-2200	
	Date November 6, 20--
PAY TO THE ORDER OF CTB --	$ 735,000.00
Seven hundred thirty-five thousand and 00/100 --- **Dollars**	
BOCA Bank & Trust	
Boca Raton, FL 33428	
MEMO Invoice 1009 less discount	*Jonathan Sanchez*
	(For Classroom Use Only)

Transaction 50 ▶ November 10

Record the transaction for deposit of a check received from Recorded Music Distributors for Invoice No. 1010, less 2% discount.

Complete the deposit ticket for November 10 transactions. Enter the check for $735,000.00 on the deposit ticket. Total the deposit ticket.

Recorded Music Distributors
8801 Creek Court
Palatine, IL 60038-8801

No. 4450   71-924
            277

Date November 8, 20--

PAY TO THE
ORDER OF CTB -- $ 735,000.00

Seven hundred thirty-five thousand and 00/100 -------------- **Dollars**

⊗**Palatine**
BANK & TRUST
Palatine, IL 60038

MEMO Invoice 1010 less discount

Frances Graves

(For Classroom Use Only)

Pay the invoice for the temporary workers.

Cortez Staffing Solutions		Invoice No.: 3898	
7753 Alan Road		Invoice Date: November 1, 20--	
Lake in the Hills, IL 60156-7753			

To:

CTB
2244 Brian Avenue
Crystal Lake, IL 60014-0065

Terms: Net 10

Quantity	Description	Unit Price	Amount
160	Yolanda Winfrey, hours worked in October	$25.00	$4,000.00
160	Saray Ponnas, hours worked in October	25.00	4,000.00
		Total Due	$8,000.00

Pay the invoice from the accountant (you) for work for the band for the month of October.

<table>
<tr><td colspan="2">Student Name
8725 Dee Way
Palatine, IL 60038-8725</td><td colspan="2" align="right">Invoice No.:   4404
Invoice Date: November 10, 20--</td></tr>
<tr><td colspan="2">To:
   CTB
   2244 Brian Avenue
   Crystal Lake, IL 60014-0065</td><td colspan="2" align="right">Terms: Net 10</td></tr>
</table>

Quantity	Description	Unit Price	Amount
140	Accounting services, hourly for October 20--	$30.00	$4,200.00
		Total Due	$4,200.00

Transaction 53 ▶ November 30

Write a check to Duncan Payroll Service for the amount of the total net earnings, $9,709.00. The employee deductions for Social Security and Medicare should be credited to Employer Taxes Payable. Federal and state income taxes should be credited to Employee Income Taxes payable. Record the payroll transaction for the pay period ending November 30 as follows:

Account	Debit	Credit
Salary Expense	$14,000.00	
Cash		$9,709.00
Employer Taxes Payable		1,071.00
Employee Income Taxes Payable		3,220.00

Also, you must record a transaction for the employer payroll tax expense.

Record the employer's portion of Social Security, Medicare, state unemployment tax, and federal unemployment tax as a debit to Employer Payable Tax Expense ($1,617.00) and a credit to Employer Taxes Payable ($1,617.00).

Duncan Payroll Service
5893 West Street
Crystal Lake, IL 60014-5893

CTB
Payroll Register
For the payroll period ending 11/30/20--

| Name | Gross Earnings | Deductions | | | | Net Earnings |
		Social Security	Medicare	Federal Income Tax	State Income Tax	
Student Name	$6,000.00	$372.00	$ 87.00	$1,200.00	$180.00	$4,161.00
Yolanda Winfrey	4,000.00	248.00	87.00	800.00	120.00	2,774.00
Saray Ponnas	4,000.00	248.00	87.00	800.00	120.00	2,774.00
Total Payroll	$14,000.00	$868.00	$203.00	$2,800.00	$420.00	$9,709.00

Employer Payroll Tax Expense:

Social Security	$ 868.00
Medicare	203.00
State Unemployment Tax	434.00
Federal Unemployment Tax	112.00
Total Employer Expense	$1,617.00

Transaction 54 ▶ November 30

Create an invoice to Vallejo Music, Inc., for the sale of CDs. Use November 30 for the date. Use Invoice No. 1011. The address is:

Vallejo Music, Inc.
8834 Trail Road
Vallejo, CA 94591-8834

The band is billing for 100,000 CDs at $10.00 each. The terms for the invoice are 2/10 Net 30.

December Transactions

Transaction 55 ▶ December 10

Record the transaction for deposit of the check received from Vallejo Music, Inc., for Invoice No. 1011, less 2% discount.

Complete a deposit ticket for the December 10 transaction. Deposit tickets are found on pages 84–87. Enter the check for $980,000.00 on the deposit ticket. Total the deposit ticket.

Vallejo Music, Inc.
8834 Trail Road
Vallejo, CA 94591-8834

No. 7890   14-114
              522

Date December 8, 20--

PAY TO THE
ORDER OF   CTB -- $ 980,000.00

Nine hundred eighty thousand and 00/100 --------- **Dollars**

VALLEJO
Bank & Trust
Vallejo, CA 94591

MEMO Invoice 1011 less discount

Juliana Santos

(For Classroom Use Only)

Write a check to Duncan Payroll Service for the CTB payroll tax liability from the November 30 payroll.

Debit Employer Taxes Payable for Social Security, Medicare, state unemployment tax, and federal unemployment tax. Debit Employee Income Taxes Payable for employee federal income tax and employee state income tax. Credit Cash for the total employer expense.

Duncan Payroll Service
5893 West Street
Crystal Lake, IL 60014-5893

CTB
Payroll Tax Liability
For the payroll period ending 11/30/20--

Employer Payroll Tax Expense:	
Social Security	$1,736.00
Medicare	406.00
Employee Federal Income Tax	2,800.00
Employee State Income Tax	420.00
State Unemployment Tax	434.00
Federal Unemployment Tax	112.00
Total Employer Expense	$5,908.00

Transaction 57 ▶ December 31

The band has played at Club Low every Friday night for the fourth quarter of the year. Create an invoice to Club Low. Use December 31 for the date. Use Invoice No. 1012. The club's address is:

Club Low
12446 Virginia Road
Crystal Lake, IL 60014-0446

The band is billing for 13 shows at $400.00 per show. The terms for the invoice are Net 30.

Transaction 58 ▶ December 31

The band has played at The Leading Edge every Saturday night for the fourth quarter of the year. Create an invoice to The Leading Edge. Use December 31 for the date. Use Invoice No. 1013. The club's address is:

The Leading Edge
1078 Virginia Road
Crystal Lake, IL 60014-1078

The band is billing for 13 shows at $400.00 per show. The terms for the invoice are Net 30.

**Accounting Tip**

See Transaction 53 to
review recording payroll
transactions.

Transaction 59 ▶ December 31

Record the payroll transaction for the pay period ending December 31, 20--.
Write a check to Duncan Payroll Service for the amount of the total net earnings. Record a transaction for the employer's payroll tax liability.

Duncan Payroll Service
5893 West Street
Crystal Lake, IL 60014-5893

CTB
Payroll Register
For the payroll period ending 12/31/20--

| Name | Gross Earnings | Deductions | | | | Net Earnings |
		Social Security	Medicare	Federal Income Tax	State Income Tax	
Student Name	$ 6,000.00	$372.00	$ 87.00	$1,200.00	$180.00	$4,161.00
Yolanda Winfrey	4,000.00	248.00	87.00	800.00	120.00	2,774.00
Saray Ponnas	4,000.00	248.00	87.00	800.00	120.00	2,774.00
Total Payroll	$14,000.00	$868.00	$203.00	$2,800.00	$420.00	$9,709.00

Employer Payroll Tax Expense:

Social Security	$ 868.00
Medicare	203.00
State Unemployment Tax	341.00
Federal Unemployment Tax	56.00
Total Employer Expense	$1,468.00

QuickBooks and *Peachtree* users: Add the name of each charity as a vendor before creating the checks. Leave the address area blank.

Transaction 60 ▶ December 31

The partners agreed to make $50,000.00 donations to five charities. Write the checks and record the transaction. (Debit Donations Expense and credit Cash.)

 MEMORANDUM

TO: Student Name

FROM: Kacy Jaffe

DATE: December 31, 20--

SUBJECT: Charitable Contributions

Please write a $50,000.00 check to each of the five charities listed below. Each band member will hand deliver a check to the charity he or she chose.

- American Cancer Society
- Habitat for Humanity International
- Mothers Against Drunk Driving
- The Nature Conservancy
- Teaching Tolerance

Thanks.

Transaction 61 ▶ December 31

The partners agreed to take a $500,000.00 distribution of earnings. Record the transaction.

MEMORANDUM

TO: Student Name

FROM: Kacy Jaffe

DATE: December 31, 20--

SUBJECT: Distribution of Profits

Please write a check for $500,000.00 to each of the five partners.

Thanks.

Accounting Tip

After completing the December transactions, compare your account balances to the check figures for October through December on pages 82 and 83.

Print a Report ▶ December 31

After you have completed all of the transactions for July through December (before adjusting entries), print a report showing transactions for July 1 through December 31, 20--.

Peachtree users: Print a General Ledger report.

QuickBooks users: Print a Journal report. Add your name in a footer on the report.

Excel users: Print the *General Ledger* page showing columns A and B and transactions for July through December. Hide columns with data that you do not wish to print. Add your name in a footer on the sheet.

Adjusting Entries ▶ December 31

Record the adjusting entries as detailed below.

1. Calculate and record a full year of depreciation expense for the office furniture. Use a ten-year life and straight-line depreciation with no salvage value.

2. Calculate and record a full year of depreciation expense for the computer and printer. Use a three-year life and straight-line depreciation with no salvage value.

3. Record amortization of capitalized studio cost of $24,125.00 for the year. (Debit Amortization Expense and credit Capitalized Studio Costs.) Also record amortization of $5,000.00 of Goodwill. (Debit Amortization Expense and credit Goodwill.)

4. There were 55,000 CDs on hand at year end. Calculate the FIFO inventory cost for the CDs at $1.25 per unit. (Credit the Cost of Goods Sold account Ending Inventory and debit the Asset account Inventory.) Read the FYI FIFO Inventory on page 78 to learn more about this inventory method.

5. Adjust Prepaid Expenses for the amount of rent expense for the year.

6. Adjust Unearned Rent for the amount of rent earned this year. Assume Park & Yung, Inc., used the studio from March through December.

7. Adjust Prepaid Expenses for the amount of electricity consumed this year. The December bill shows a $100.00 credit. (Debit Utilities Expense for the amount consumed.)

8. Adjust Prepaid Expenses for the amount of telephone expense for the year. The December bill shows a $75.00 credit. (Debit Utilities Expense for the amount consumed.)

9. Record the interest income ($14,960.00) earned on the checking account for the year. (Debit Cash and credit Interest Income.)

Accounting Tip

Excel users: Remember to record the interest income amount on the last check stub.

Accounting Tip

After completing the adjusting transactions, compare your account balances to the check figures on pages 82 and 83.

Print Income Statement ▶ December 31

When you have completed the adjusting entries, prepare an income statement.

Peachtree users: Use the date range December 1, 20-- to December 31, 20-- for the report. The report will show the current month (December) and the year-to-date figures.

QuickBooks users: Select January 1 and December 31 of the current year for the From and To dates. Add your name in a footer on the report.

Excel users: Add your name in a footer on the *Income Statement* sheet. Print the sheet.

FIFO Inventory

FIFO stands for *first in, first out.* FIFO refers to a method for handling inventory. With this method, inventory is sold in the order that it is purchased or produced. This method is consistent with the way inventory flows through many businesses.

Companies that use FIFO inventory should keep detailed records of all inventory purchased or sold. Without detailed records, accurately calculating inventory cost would not be possible.

When inventory is sold, the cost of goods sold may include individual items at two or more costs. As with other inventory methods, doing periodic counts to maintain the accuracy of inventory records is important.

To calculate inventory cost using the FIFO method, multiply the number of units on hand by the purchase/production cost of the units on hand. See the following example:

Units on hand at year end from purchases on 8/30 and 9/30	1,000
Cost per unit of 500 units purchased on 9/30	$2.00
Cost per unit of 500 units purchased on 8/30	$1.75

500 × $2.00 = $1,000.00
500 × $1.75 = $ 875.00
$1,000.00 + $875.00 = $1,875.00 FIFO Inventory Cost

Closing Entries ▶ December 31

Record the closing entries for CTB.

Net income should total $4,102,045.83. This amount cannot be divided evenly by five. Distribute the amount among the five partners as follows:

Name	Amount
Kyle Jaffe	$820,409.17
Kacy Jaffe	$820,409.17
Bernadette Yap	$820,409.17
Joey Yap	$820,409.16
Ian Morris	$820,409.16

Peachtree and *QuickBooks* users: Print a Trial Balance report for use in making closing entries.

Excel users: Use the amounts in the General Ledger, Account Balances After Adjustments column to determine amounts for the closing entries.

Print a Report ▶ December 31

After you have completed all of the adjusting and closing transactions, print a report that shows these transactions.

Peachtree users: Print a General Ledger report. Use December 31, 20-- for both the From and To dates.

QuickBooks users: Print a Journal report. Use December 31, 20-- for both the From and To dates. Add your name in a footer on the report.

Excel users: Print the *General Ledger* page showing columns A and B and the last five columns of the worksheet, columns BL through BP. Hide columns that you do not wish to print. Add your name in a footer on the sheet.

Financial Statements ▶ December 31

Print financial statements as directed for your software below. The amounts in these reports are generated automatically by the software, based on the transactions you have recorded.

Peachtree users: View a Balance Sheet report as of December 31, 20--. Print the report.

QuickBooks users: View a Balance Sheet report as of December 31, 20--. Add your name in a footer line. Print the report. View a Statement of Cash Flows report for the year ended December 31, 20--. Add your name in a footer line. Print the report.

Excel users: Enter your name in a footer on the *Balance Sheet, Owner's Equity*, and *Cash Flows* sheets. Print these sheets.

Statement of Cash Flows Report

During operation of a business, money is received and paid out for many reasons. A Statement of Cash Flows report shows the increases and decreases in the Cash account for a stated period. This report is used by managers to help determine how well a company is doing.

There are three types of activities that affect cash flow:

1. Operating Activities—transactions that affect net income. Examples include the purchase and sale of inventory.

2. Investing Activities—transactions that affect the investment in noncurrent assets. Examples include the purchase and sale of fixed or plant assets.

3. Financing Activities—transactions that affect long-term liabilities or owner's equity. Examples include borrowing money and partner drawing.

If more cash is received than is paid out (positive cash flow), managers can purchase new assets to maintain or expand the business. If more cash is paid out than is received (negative cash flow), managers may need to reduce costs or delay replacing assets.

If you are using *Excel* or *QuickBooks*, look at the transactions in the three categories on the Statement of Cash Flows.

Check Figures

You can check your progress by comparing your account balances to the check figures shown on the following two pages. Check figures show the year-to-date balances at the end of March, June, September, and December (before adjusting entries). Check figures are also provided for account balances after adjusting entries and after closing entries. For example, when you have completed the last transaction for March, the balance of the Cash account should be $2,600.00 as shown in the Jan.–Mar. Year-to-Date column. Credit balances are shown in parentheses.

Credit amounts are shown in parentheses.

No.	Account	Jan.–Mar. Year-to-Date	Apr.–Jun. Year-to-Date	Jul.–Sep. Year-to-Date	Before Adj. Oct.–Dec. Year-to-Date	Account Balance After Adjustments	12/31 Ending Balance
	Current Assets						
1105	Cash	2,600.00	51,950.00	1,800,400.00	1,443,674.00	1,458,634.00	1,458,634.00
1107	Accounts Receivable	50,400.00	10,400.00	10,400.00	10,400.00	10,400.00	10,400.00
1115	Inventory	0.00	0.00	0.00	0.00	68,750.00	68,750.00
1120	Prepaid Deposits	100.00	100.00	100.00	100.00	100.00	100.00
1125	Prepaid Expenses	11,900.00	11,900.00	13,400.00	13,400.00	175.00	175.00
	Plant Assets						
1205	Computer Equipment	4,816.24	4,816.24	4,816.24	4,816.24	4,816.24	4,816.24
1210	Acc. Depr.—Comp. Equipment	0.00	0.00	0.00	0.00	(1,605.41)	(1,605.41)
1215	Office Furniture	2,400.00	2,400.00	2,400.00	2,400.00	2,400.00	2,400.00
1220	Acc. Depr.—Office Furniture	0.00	0.00	0.00	0.00	(240.00)	(240.00)
	Other Assets						
1305	Capitalized Studio Costs	48,700.00	48,700.00	48,700.00	48,700.00	24,575.00	24,575.00
1310	Goodwill	20,000.00	20,000.00	20,000.00	20,000.00	15,000.00	15,000.00
	Current Liabilities						
2105	Accounts Payable	0.00	0.00	0.00	0.00	0.00	0.00
2110	Employer Taxes Payable	0.00	0.00	0.00	(2,539.00)	(2,539.00)	(2,539.00)
2115	Employee Income Taxes Payable	0.00	0.00	0.00	(3,220.00)	(3,220.00)	(3,220.00)
2120	Unearned Rent	(1,200.00)	(1,200.00)	(1,200.00)	(1,200.00)	(200.00)	(200.00)
	Long-Term Liability						
2205	Loan Payable	(12,000.00)	(12,000.00)	0.00	0.00	0.00	0.00
	Owner's Equity						
3105	Kyle Jaffe, Capital	(20,000.00)	(20,000.00)	(20,000.00)	(20,000.00)	(20,000.00)	(315,409.17)
3110	Kyle Jaffe, Drawing	0.00	0.00	25,000.00	525,000.00	525,000.00	0.00
3115	Kacy Jaffe, Capital	(20,000.00)	(20,000.00)	(20,000.00)	(20,000.00)	(20,000.00)	(315,409.17)
3120	Kacy Jaffe, Drawing	0.00	0.00	25,000.00	525,000.00	525,000.00	0.00
3125	Bernadette Yap, Capital	(20,000.00)	(20,000.00)	(20,000.00)	(20,000.00)	(20,000.00)	(315,409.17)
3130	Bernadette Yap, Drawing	0.00	0.00	25,000.00	525,000.00	525,000.00	0.00
3135	Joey Yap, Capital	(20,000.00)	(20,000.00)	(20,000.00)	(20,000.00)	(20,000.00)	(315,409.16)
3140	Joey Yap, Drawing	0.00	0.00	25,000.00	525,000.00	525,000.00	0.00
3145	Ian Morris, Capital	(20,000.00)	(20,000.00)	(20,000.00)	(20,000.00)	(20,000.00)	(315,409.16)
3150	Ian Morris, Drawing	0.00	0.00	25,000.00	525,000.00	525,000.00	0.00
3195	Income Summary	0.00	0.00	0.00	0.00	0.00	0.00

CHECK FIGURES

Credit amounts are shown in parentheses.

No.	Account	Jan.–Mar. Year-to-Date	Apr.–Jun. Year-to-Date	Jul.–Sep. Year-to-Date	Before Adj. Oct.–Dec. Year-to-Date	Account Balance After Adjustments	12/31 Ending Balance
	Sales						
4105	CD Sales	(40,000.00)	(40,000.00)	(2,840,000.00)	(5,340,000.00)	(5,340,000.00)	0.00
4110	CD Sales Discount	0.00	0.00	56,000.00	106,000.00	106,000.00	0.00
4115	Club Show Income	(10,400.00)	(20,800.00)	(31,200.00)	(41,600.00)	(41,600.00)	0.00
	Cost of Goods Sold						
5102	Beginning Inventory	0.00	0.00	0.00	0.00	0.00	0.00
5105	Purchases	22,500.00	22,500.00	847,500.00	847,500.00	847,500.00	0.00
5110	Purchases Discount	0.00	0.00	(7,500.00)	(7,500.00)	(7,500.00)	0.00
5115	Ending Inventory	0.00	0.00	0.00	0.00	(68,750.00)	0.00
	Expenses						
6105	Advertising Expense	0.00	0.00	6,000.00	21,000.00	21,000.00	0.00
6110	Amortization Expense	0.00	0.00	0.00	0.00	29,125.00	0.00
6115	Depr. Exp.—Computer Equipment	0.00	0.00	0.00	0.00	1,605.41	0.00
6120	Depr. Exp.—Office Furniture	0.00	0.00	0.00	0.00	240.00	0.00
6125	Donations Expense	0.00	0.00	0.00	250,000.00	250,000.00	0.00
6130	Employer Payroll Taxes Expense	0.00	0.00	0.00	3,085.00	3,085.00	0.00
6135	Office Workers Expense	0.00	1,050.00	18,250.00	45,050.00	45,050.00	0.00
6140	Rent Expense	0.00	0.00	0.00	0.00	8,400.00	0.00
6145	Salary Expense	0.00	0.00	0.00	28,000.00	28,000.00	0.00
6150	Security Expense	0.00	0.00	26,000.00	26,000.00	26,000.00	0.00
6155	Supplies Expense	183.76	183.76	183.76	183.76	183.76	0.00
6160	Utilities Expense	0.00	0.00	0.00	0.00	4,825.00	0.00
	Other Income						
7105	Rent Income	0.00	0.00	0.00	0.00	(1,000.00)	0.00
7110	Interest Income	0.00	0.00	0.00	0.00	(14,960.00)	0.00
	Other Expense						
8105	Interest Expense	0.00	0.00	750.00	750.00	750.00	0.00

Deposit Tickets

Deposit Ticket

CTB
2244 Brian Avenue
Crystal Lake, IL 60014-0065
Account No. 43-452119

DATE _____

Deposits may not be available for immediate withdrawal.

⭐ All Star Bank
Crystal Lake, IL 60014

Currency		
Coin		
Checks		
Total Deposit		

List additional checks on back.

(For Classroom Use Only)

Deposit Ticket

CTB
2244 Brian Avenue
Crystal Lake, IL 60014-0065
Account No. 43-452119

DATE _____

Deposits may not be available for immediate withdrawal.

⭐ All Star Bank
Crystal Lake, IL 60014

Currency		
Coin		
Checks		
Total Deposit		

List additional checks on back.

(For Classroom Use Only)

Deposit Ticket

CTB
2244 Brian Avenue
Crystal Lake, IL 60014-0065
Account No. 43-452119

DATE _____

Deposits may not be available for immediate withdrawal.

⭐ All Star Bank
Crystal Lake, IL 60014

Currency		
Coin		
Checks		
Total Deposit		

List additional checks on back.

(For Classroom Use Only)

Deposit Ticket

CTB
2244 Brian Avenue
Crystal Lake, IL 60014-0065
Account No. 43-452119

DATE _____

Deposits may not be available for immediate withdrawal.

⭐ All Star Bank
Crystal Lake, IL 60014

Currency		
Coin		
Checks		
Total Deposit		

List additional checks on back.

(For Classroom Use Only)

Deposit Ticket

CTB
2244 Brian Avenue
Crystal Lake, IL 60014-0065
Account No. 43-452119

DATE _____

Deposits may not be available for immediate withdrawal.

⭐ All Star Bank
Crystal Lake, IL 60014

Currency		
Coin		
Checks		
Total Deposit		

List additional checks on back.

(For Classroom Use Only)

Deposit Ticket

CTB
2244 Brian Avenue
Crystal Lake, IL 60014-0065
Account No. 43-452119

DATE _____

Deposits may not be available for immediate withdrawal.

⭐ All Star Bank
Crystal Lake, IL 60014

Currency		
Coin		
Checks		
Total Deposit		

List additional checks on back.

(For Classroom Use Only)

Deposit Ticket

CTB
2244 Brian Avenue
Crystal Lake, IL 60014-0065
Account No. 43-452119

DATE _____

Deposits may not be available for immediate withdrawal.

All Star Bank
Crystal Lake, IL 60014

Currency		
Coin		
Checks		
Total Deposit		

List additional checks on back.

(For Classroom Use Only)

Deposit Ticket

CTB
2244 Brian Avenue
Crystal Lake, IL 60014-0065
Account No. 43-452119

DATE _____

Deposits may not be available for immediate withdrawal.

All Star Bank
Crystal Lake, IL 60014

Currency		
Coin		
Checks		
Total Deposit		

List additional checks on back.

(For Classroom Use Only)

Deposit Ticket

CTB
2244 Brian Avenue
Crystal Lake, IL 60014-0065
Account No. 43-452119

DATE _____

Deposits may not be available for immediate withdrawal.

All Star Bank
Crystal Lake, IL 60014

Currency		
Coin		
Checks		
Total Deposit		

List additional checks on back.

(For Classroom Use Only)

Deposit Ticket

CTB
2244 Brian Avenue
Crystal Lake, IL 60014-0065
Account No. 43-452119

DATE _____

Deposits may not be available for immediate withdrawal.

All Star Bank
Crystal Lake, IL 60014

Currency		
Coin		
Checks		
Total Deposit		

List additional checks on back.

(For Classroom Use Only)

Deposit Ticket

CTB
2244 Brian Avenue
Crystal Lake, IL 60014-0065
Account No. 43-452119

DATE _____

Deposits may not be available for immediate withdrawal.

All Star Bank
Crystal Lake, IL 60014

Currency		
Coin		
Checks		
Total Deposit		

List additional checks on back.

(For Classroom Use Only)

Deposit Ticket

CTB
2244 Brian Avenue
Crystal Lake, IL 60014-0065
Account No. 43-452119

DATE _____

Deposits may not be available for immediate withdrawal.

All Star Bank
Crystal Lake, IL 60014

Currency		
Coin		
Checks		
Total Deposit		

List additional checks on back.

(For Classroom Use Only)